G000272543

Reason has its place in life — and so does living. has its place in reason.

Let loving be a bridge between what is and what ought to be — so that heart and mind can march together in search of the future.

ROY FULLER

NEW POEMS

Poems can be the bullets to wreck the past
in favour of the future — but as for Fuller,
we shall see, we shall see . . . .

Also by Roy Fuller

★

Poetry

POEMS
THE MIDDLE OF A WAR
A LOST SEASON
EPITAPHS AND OCCASIONS
COUNTERPARTS
BRUTUS'S ORCHARD
COLLECTED POEMS 1936–1961
BUFF

Novels

WITH MY LITTLE EYE
THE SECOND CURTAIN
FANTASY AND FUGUE
IMAGE OF A SOCIETY
THE RUINED BOYS
THE FATHER'S COMEDY
THE PERFECT FOOL
MY CHILD, MY SISTER

For Children

SAVAGE GOLD
CATSPAW

ROY FULLER

NEW POEMS

Ein Räthsel ist Reinentsprungenes. Auch
Der Gesang kaum darf es enthüllen. Denn
Wie du anfiengst, wirst du bleiben.
HÖLDERLIN

A mystery are those of pure origin.
Even song may hardly unveil it.
For as you began, so you will remain.
TRANSLATION BY MICHAEL HAMBURGER

ANDRE DEUTSCH

FIRST PUBLISHED 1968 BY
ANDRE DEUTSCH LIMITED
105 GREAT RUSSEL STREET
LONDON WCI
COPYRIGHT © 1968 BY ROY FULLER
SECOND IMPRESSION JANUARY 1969
ALL RIGHTS RESERVED
PRINTED IN GREAT BRITAIN BY
EBENEZER BAYLIS & SON LTD
THE TRINITY PRESS
WORCESTER AND LONDON
SBN 233 96025 2

To Jennifer Ross, with affection
and in gratitude for *The London Magazine*

Contents

ROY FULLER

NEW POEMS

THE PAINTER

You object: the paintings are not for the mass
Though I've chosen for models those exhausted by labour
Or worn out by a life of shame – having at first
Been preoccupied with dancers and thoroughbreds.

Well-taken point: few can stand seeing their arses
From a low, rearward view; or like having fixed
The moment when no amount of scrubbing
Seems to remove the ingrained dirt from the knee-cap.

But one wished to exclude the enviable element
Inherent in horses and girls. And you can't
Have art be about nothing. Hence these saddles
Of fat, these toilets we devote so much time to.

Wouldn't I really have wished my technique
To be put to the service of princes' triumphal entries
Or the death of God? Better still, perhaps,
For it to have accompanied dreadful emotions.

Yet to get down the bowlishness of zinc bowls
And the way the nature of zinc presses against
The nerve-ends of organic life – something,
In these days of bureaucracy and the re-arming Huns.

THE SYMPHONIST

To write just too many symphonies
For the memory easily to
Identify; to have made love to
Her in a variety of strange
Rooms and woods; to dream of clear meanings,
And on waking utterly forget . . .

Is it the Sixth where the initial
Largo is chased by two raspberry-
Blowing rondos? And the Ninth programmed
The withstanding of the seige of the
Boulevarded city by heroes,
Or the gazing at a young harpist.

In some uneasy interlude of
Peace the lake fell. Embedded in its
Strata was her skull, exemplar of
Eye-ridges on their way to thinking.
For 300,000 years or so
The axe-heads scarcely altered their shape.

Then the dream was recalled. It involved
Rolling fire on the far-off plain,
A flight in which she was left behind.
Out of that agony of loss sprang
A score for a thousand voices, and
Seventeen years of complete silence.

Think of quite outrageous conjunctions.
Have the tympani slogged during the
Viola's cadenza. Enfold in
The long hirsute arms two tender breasts
And a white rib-cage unfitted for
A time of ice, of philistine rule.

To make four movements out of four notes;
To end with a transformation of
An early, almost forgotten theme;
To devote a whole life to wordless
Communication . . . Trumpeters, where
Are your ox-horns? Girls, your rouge for bones?

THE ART OF THE APPLE

The apple, stolid centre of assemblies
Of bottle, napkin, pipe, assumes in autumn
A more active role in art by casting
A pointilliste shadow for its tree, composed of
    Blobs: green, blush-red, rotten-brown.

What forces you, apple-tree, to become a firework,
Throwing up coloured orbs that stay suspended –
The previous shower, not all extinguished,
Still on the ground; is your cylinder hollow,
    In fact, though so gnarled and dense?

'Draw lines; whether from memory or after
Nature. Then you will be a good artist.' Thus
Ingres to Degas. The apple-tree is about
To reveal the rectilinear essence
    Of its vague superstructure.

Confusing conspectus of periods and
Schools, how can we make up our minds about you?
Even plucking the compact heart from your depths
And biting its blend of flesh and sinew, sweet
    And tart, leaves us uncertain.

Some monk in a past century grafted on,
Perhaps, to the original feeble crab
A vision of blossoming stigmata and
Miraculous food. One finds suspiciously
    Romantic the concept now.

SINFONIA A GRAN ORQUESTA

Feeling my heart about to accelerate,
I swallow a pill of phenobarbitone.
Odd how one enjoys the bitterness, knowing
It will fade, as will the cutting edge from the
    World of ludicrous anxieties.

But not that world only contains the destructive
Bodies, of course: waiting the normal, I play
The Ariaga symphony; the boy dead
Of Koch's bacillus at nineteen, at the door
    Of an epoch of relative calm.

Though how can one measure the effect on the
Metabolism or on the corpuscles'
Resistance of a long campaign of burning
And rape? Staggering indeed that should be shaped
    At all the score's industrious lines.

For the heart's increased action attempts in vain
To keep up with the interpretation to
Itself of an age of nonchalance to art.
Before we sleep, the throbbing horns underline
    A tune of complete irrelevance.

One wrote to me out of the blue: 'Dear comrade . . .'
Touched at the address, after thirty-five years,
I replied, found he believed in a divine
Intervention in human affairs at this
    Stage of almost complete disaster.

Is it weakness that makes me curiously
Not unsympathetic to the notion that
In a century of culture's sickliness
Something is working on the other side – that its
    Death is a required prelude, in fact?

[15]

No, but the goodness of the gods cannot be
Counted on. They came once before, grey-eyed or
Bird-shaped, and through those they were enamoured of
Imparted such secrets as optical columns
    Surrounding an evident justice.

Nevertheless, comrade, one is not compelled
To envisage ruined pantheons stretching
To eternity, agreed. Moreover, one
Can enjoy the bitterness, waiting for the
    Oppressed libido to take over.

CHINOISERIE

I've always been comfortably off.
In my poorer days my desires were modest:
Now I earn more, my previous habits
Circumscribe the area of my extravagance.
I've tried to take care that being a poet
Didn't get in the way of my making a living,
And eventually this other occupation
Actually incremented my income
And stopped hurting my respectability.
It's a toss up whether I turn first
To the literary or the financial page,
And I find it just as painful to read
Of a bonus issue of shares I failed to buy
As of the success of a rival writer.
Yet I can seriously assert
That finally money doesn't matter.
It's supported a life I can't approve of:
I've saved it for a life I shall never enjoy.
Like my neatness and punctuality,
My interest in it denotes a fixation
At the irrelevant anal stage of existence.
If I became penniless tomorrow . . .
Still impossible to change to a hero of art!
An incurable lack of high seriousness
Is indicated by concern about cash;
A deficiency in the religious sense;
A fatal practicality for life.
Given this species of character,
My follies have arisen from denying it –
Underestimating the greed of others,
And the longevity of capitalism.
How much happier I'd have been
Had I put my patrimony in low-yielders,
And been less timid and considerate,
And voted Tory, and stuck to prose.

READING *THE BOSTONIANS* IN
ALGECIRAS BAY

To Alan Ross

At the next table, on the terrace
(*The Bostonians* open on my
Knee), a pale pumice domineering
Head; in the prosperous buttonhole
An order. Behind the lush hotel,
Folds of burnt-brown, donkey-littered hills,
Beyond which runs the river with the
Battle-name. Old man, did you, thirty
Years ago, fire the shot that killed my friend?

'Whatever money was given her
She gave it away to a negro
Or a refugee. No woman could
Be less invidious, but on the
Whole she preferred these two classes of
The human race.' Though even Henry
Found history grave at last; came to
The 'unspeakable give-away of
The whole fool's paradise of our past.'

On the concrete sheds by the quayside:
PESCADOS S. L., dominating
The life of the town, arsehole of Spain.
In this suburb, round the stinking stream,
An African poverty, from which
The boys emerge, asking for 'money',
Threatening with the mock horns of bulls,
Plucking a pack of Marlboro from
The breast pocket of my ink voile shirt.

Despite the cigarette-evidenced
Yankee subventions, only the jail
And the *plaza de toros* look clean
And in the least substantially built.
And to guarantee the lottery's
Success there are inexhaustible
Supplies of the wall-eyed and crippled
To be led to street-corners by boys
And there reassure the unlucky.

Dear friend, all is still to struggle for.
In our middle-age what engrosses
Is the play of human emotions –
In the hotel today, a wedding:
A girl of eleven perturbed at
Her mother wearing only one glove,
Dusting down her elder sister's dress;
Though herself bustless. Illustrative
The guests, of all stages in love's game.

But in that room of our chance meeting
Over the crumby Piccadilly
Of 1944 – did we think
Then to succumb to slide-rule metrics,
Hear social-democratic England
Object to the roasting merely of
Civilians in yet another
Civil war, and to stay *de luxe* in
The realms of a tyrant of our youth?

It's not enough to have chosen
The figurative (and preferably
Front view) to hang on our walls, alas!
Nor to have laughed over luncheon at
Numerous other *littérateurs*;

Borne the mediaeval and junkie
Blend of today's medical science;
Nor even, in your case, to have slaved
At friendship, and support of the arts.

What a mess, societies of men!
At first spreading out along these coasts,
Leaving their driftwood and turds afloat,
Amphorae capsized by sand, pillars
Broken, democratic orations
Echoing hollowly to lands of
Fog – where, posed as abstract principles,
The punks of a class's lust gather
A patina of factory grime.

As well as with unrequited love,
Dying, and distaste for our own verse,
Shall we always have to put up with
Delusions induced by the very
Apparatus intended to cure –
Sick doctors, nurses with biceps,
And inside the asylum's high walls
Its own individual banner?
Yes, in our time; and in our sons' time.

ASTAPOVO, 1910

The old man who died at the railway
Station, ready to leave for somewhere
Else, said: 'Whoever is happy is
Right.' The birch groves silvered the land to
Asia, and the peasants were about
To throw in their lot with factory
Hands and the cheesed-off military.

But at the moment he was fleeing
A marital sexuality
Turned grotesque with age. Locomotives
With top-hats for funnels, that had run
Down Anna Karenina, passed to
And fro while he lay dying, dreaming
Of the end of all authority.

His diary was found to observe:
'Only old people and children, free
From sexual lusts, live a true life.'
No doubt he was off to find it. The
Rest of humanity, he believed,
Was merely a factory for the
Continuation of animals.

Utopian textile mills, cigar
Smoking women, students with grenades
Tagged 'Czar', apostles of deep breathing,
Vegetarianism – all these
Had to flourish and then be subsumed
In the amendment of bankers' aims
And an electrical policy.

'Many people think that poetry
May be found only in sexual
Life. All true poetry is always
Outside it.' One sees what he meant, though
Reluctantly disagreeing. Make
Poetry out of this, said the head
Of heavy industry, with reason.

Each generation is unhappy
In its own way; looks on its children
With complacent envy. 'For you we
Expropriated the unjust and
Rich. Why aren't you laughing?' But the young
Feel no more than poets and old men
That matters accord with their vision.

THE MAP

A brilliant conjecture indeed,
Where the very shape of our wishes –
Innocence-smooth belly-curve of coast
And single deep safe inlet for our vessel –
Was adumbrated from mere glimpses
Across impossible seas. Peaks rose
From hinterlands of ignorant white,
Twins dimly familiar from childhood;
And even the capricious climate,
The zinc veins, croppable savannahs,
And fern grottos diamonded by torrents
Were indicated on succeeding
Folios. But what are these added
In the margin? Mere fancies of the
Cartographer or croakings of some
Returned, stick-limbed, insane explorer?
Farting winds from gross cheeks of cherubs
Blow trivial devils to the Poles,
Arses revealed by tattered small-clothes.
Supporting the whole, a recumbent
Skeleton, detached fore index joint
Reflectively along a toothy jaw
From which on a scroll the legend winds:
New Found Land, graveyard of fat monsters –
Anchorage ice-locked at all seasons –
Loud gales, crabs in lichen, smell of fish.

ON THE RAILWAY PLATFORM

Infant on the railway platform, whose
Head as I pass I dare to impress
With a communicating finger,
This Mad Hatter figure scarcely knows
Whether he longs for your innocence
Or the youth of your nearby mother
Or a generalised human love.

Encountering you again in my
Pacings, I quite needlessly enquire
About the cardboard carton you clutch
Of veritable Dolly Mixtures.
A gleam of detached amusement fails
To check your search for the train that you
Conceive will appear close to the ground –

And rightly so, I admit, thinking
The matter over as later I
Repose my bowler upon the rack,
And settle to perusing *The Times*.
Beware, child, of your hand in crazy
Crashing doors and of ostensibly
Benevolent, unknown gentlemen.

CREEPER

A tendril's actually entered
The house, and faintly tinted it is
(A sinew or duct from deep inside
Some anatomy) compared to the
Shining magenta leaves on the wall.

These, hung in September stillness, have
Made the yellow brickwork reflect their
Flushing; and at death's approach, lesser
Leaves having fallen, show the tangled
Cordage with which they have been hoisted.

Probing filament, what do you seek
In our affairs? You have waited too
Long to arrive, in any event,
For your pallid reach must fail soon, not
Even leave a dry whisker, perhaps.

What a frail representative of
That serrate, cinquefoil splendour! Yet it
Can be seen that even the foetus
Shapes along your lank length have the same
Strange oneness of contour and number.

Undoubtedly in a season of
Dying the preparation, though much
Of it abortive, is for re-birth;
However perverse the confidence,
And grotesque the sacrifice of flesh.

Doesn't that reassure the body's
House, invaded by extending rods
Of foreign or unruly objects?
Or merely remind our furniture
Of the restless empire of nature?

[25]

AMBIGUITIES OF TRAVEL

And will you really wake at the hotel
With the mountain in the garden and the crippled
Gardener? And go to see the wall-paintings
Of the wall-eyed flautists, and the pink sandstone
Water nymph with vulva-exposing embroideries,
And the silk banner (reconstruction) of Lord Kanishka?

Poetry is something between the dream
And its interpretation. Through pleached boughs
Of blossoming, still vivid your pantisocratic
Imaginings, how hurtful to think
Of the past dragging its foot to meet you,
As though a mirror stood at the pathway's end.

A saying of Kanishka: 'Human love –
So much beauty lavished on so much goodness.'
Dear child, it's only that the colours have flaked
That the musicians are so repulsive;
And the sepulchre of the ruler was long ago
Shat on by pillaging baboons.

What song will your mind rehearse as, shaving,
You see the girl still slumbering in the striped light?
That late sonata movement where, trilling each note,
The performer's hands move farther and farther apart?
Strange, both expounding life in likenesses,
Voyaging through the other's boiling wake.

MY DEAD BROTHERS

When the soothsayer spoke of my three brothers
I smiled in my sleeve, since I had only one –
   Later recalled those two dead
   Babes, their lives measured in days.

Where are you now, you strong men who would have looked
Up to me? The little lives followed so close
   On my own I could well have
   Smothered them in my cradle.

And I can even remember their names, which
They scarcely used. Would they have had my gift for
   Affairs, for art, such as it
   Is; my filbert nails, my moles?

To die before my mother and father was
Your legendary fate, my own to prove so
   Unconsolatory in
   Surviving them one by one.

The tiny internal flaw that destroyed your
Perfect appearances, how could I fail to
   Inherit, since I possess
   Such an assortment myself?

Fifty years in your graves, you rise up in the
Live wax of the hour of your births. Did you
   Sacrifice your kingdom
   For my pre-destined neurosis?

HEREDITY

Mother, it was this, then, you suffered from in
The days of my uncaring adolescence –
This unpleasant and chronic but curable,
It's said, imbalance of metabolism.

How it would have distressed you to discover
That with your timid heart you'd also passed on
A gland too officious, since only the nice
Lessons of life were to be learnt in your school.

You'd have foolishly liked to bear my symptoms
As well, to save me the trouble, just as now
(Though with rather less theoretical risk)
I'd prefer to have been the unlucky one.

Widowed, lacking the consolations of art,
How did you stand the long years of uncertain
Diagnosis, the ineffective drugs, and
Lastly the blundering knife of that epoch?

Well, you survived. And death was still a decade
Away. When it came, I was then fully seised
Of its threat, its grip, its method of bringing
Itself into life, premature grave-breath, bones –

Closer myself to the state of receiving
It. But how far then compared with the present!
Strange we should each get our wish to endure for
The other; or must the same blood expect to?

IN MEMORY OF MY CAT, DOMINO:
1951–66

Rising at dawn to pee, I thought I saw you
Curved in a chair, with head raised to look at me,
As you did at such hours. But the next moment,
More used to the gloom, there was only a jar
And a face-cloth. Time enough, nonetheless,
For love's responsibilities to return
To me.
             The unique character of the dead
Is the source of our sense of mourning and loss;
So, back in bed, I avoided calling up
What I know is intact in my mind, your life,
Entirely possessed as it was by my care.

I could conceive you not as dead but merely
Gone before me to a world that sends to us
Decreasing intimations of its beings –
No doubt because they find us in the end
Pathetic, worthy, but of small importance.

So long had we been together it never
Occurred to me I might fall somewhat behind.
Even when, familiar fur in my hands,
The sickly wave of barbiturate rose up,
I thought it was I who was journeying on –
But looking back there is only emptiness,
Your dusty medicaments and my portrait
Taken with you: sad mode of life you've outpaced.

TO A RECENTLY-ACQUIRED OMEGA

Had we been travelling together
At the limit of velocity
By now we should have made our escape
From the stacked dish-shaped dominions
Of the vassals of the sun, en route
To the nearest star. Several such
Fireballs we'd flash through arm in arm
And then, close companion, you'd soar
Yoked loosely to an archipelago
Of bones until yourself stopped beating,
Long before quitting our galaxy
Let alone reaching the vast Chelsea
Bun in Andromeda – that smear I
Search for in vain with this gun-layer's
Telescope of the last war but one,
Brass white elephant of the junk shops.

Still, even you, viable within
Less frighteningly narrow limits,
Would never survive through such space,
As you now have the chance to, the risks
Of existence and die of worn cogs.
And time is the only measure we'll
Step of any significance. Time
Of the piddling order that prompts me
To come in from the terrace, with its
Awning of myth, to the perception
Of danger to loved organisms.
Death's vacancy unvisited yet;
Unplumbed the possibility of
Resurrection, after two thousand
Million years, on other shores; unknown
The meaning of a cosmos poisoned
By the stale fall-out of explosions

Occurring in actual nature.

But during that fantastic journey
Wouldn't we have seen in retrospect
That our earth was Elysium
After all – dust without parallel,
Miraculously clouded? The dead
Regretting the passing of disease.

METAMORPHOSES

The girl in trousers wheeling a red baby
Stops to look in the window of a bread-shop.
One wants to tell her that it's all steam-
Baked muck, but really there's no chance
Of stopping her buying a bogus
Farm-house cob. Reassuring to think
That anyway it will be transformed
To wholesome milk, just as somehow she
Has gathered herself together from
The chaos of parturition and
Appears now with a lacquered bouffant
Top-knot and her old wiles unimpaired.
Why should one trouble to disguise the
Origin of the terrifying
Earth-mother, that lies in wait for men
With her odours of bergamot and
Plasma, and her soft rind filled with tripes?

STRANGE CHILD

Couldn't you think, watching the child's grave interest
In behaviour, particularly the bad
Behaviour of her near contemporaries,
That a spirit from elsewhere informed her?

Certainly the erect tower of vertebrae,
The upper lip lifted from really too tiny pearls,
The weeping hair, do not contradict the notion.

Of course, it will leave her, the ghost, to allow her
To divide into the complexities of girlhood.
But for the moment it says: 'Yes, this is what our order
Is like, you imperfect ones, intruders in nature.'
And stretches miraculous young vegetables of fingers.

Some day someone will see again in her
This utter purity, these extensions of mind
In hair, mouth, limbs – himself possessed by a demon
Of most noble generosity, fleeting domain.

ROMANCE

Girl with fat legs, reading Georgette Heyer,
Shall I arrange you in my pantheon?
Only the inspiration may be lacking,
Not your worthiness – for the preponderance
Of evidence favours the viability
Of even chinless countenances,
Just as the mousy day in April counts
In the reckoning of an empire's fall or a life
Consumed by art and syphilitic sores.
Besides, the next moment a shaft of sunlight breaks
Through southering clouds and on your betrothal finger
Illumines the diamond from Saqui & Lawrence.

Absorbed by later variations, we forget
How plain the theme was. Though planned for ultimate
Unhappiness, a world was toyed with once
Of giants mating, dropping their young
After gestations easy and prolonged
As mammoths'.
     Perhaps the trouble was
That even those sleepers in down-long barrows
Longed for a paradigm of grace,
And artists, chasing the deer's legs of their own
Genes' deviation, sealed the fatal heresy.

But when the Muse of thirteen and a half relented
She proved to be slattern and promiscuous;
And no one would buy her portrait, nude though it was –
Melted chocolate on a couch of boiled-sweet green.

Return, great goddesses, and your society
Where even little girls develop
Strong superegos, and the misfortune
Of woman's weak moral nature is unknown;

And the wars are waged on a lower epicycle
By armour diminutive as stag-beetles;
And poets forbidden to sing of their diseases
Or amatory botherations;
And only with end-stopped irony.

ROAD SAFETY

'Watch my behind not her's.' Yes, I can just read
The insolent and meant to be witty plate
On the car in front – wearing my spectacles,
Of course, and by gum it confirms what I have
Often thought: I shall crash looking at a girl,
Like some mad three-badge stoker choked by his own
Crapulous vomit. But as soon as I vow
To myself to mend my ludicrous habits
The thought arises of inexhaustible
Generations achieving the age of eye-
Catching nubility. Die happy, old boy,
If you can at all contrive to die before
The malignancies of flesh and of the State
Gouge out the gazing and its bonanza mine.

MIND TO BODY

Awake already, can't you sleep again?
Strange body, how you fail to serve the mind
That wishes above all to be the puissant prince
Of sensual indolent extremities!
I see your legs emerging from the rich
Humus of dreams, in some way anxious for
Frustrated action, botched creativity,
In a dawn inhabited only by moths and owls.

At times of physical pain one is convinced
That what is happening is happening to
Another body – that merely passing chance
Has hooked up the throbbing circuit to one's own
Perception. Likely to be a sad affair,
Lean flesh, our final reconciliation.

IN LAMBETH PALACE ROAD

Not far, as the pigeon flies, from Waterloo,
Where droppings are thick under glass awnings,
To the roadway outside St. Thomas' Hospital
On which a pigeon is smeared as on a slide,
To patients a supererogatory reminder.

How quickly a habit is established in
A strange parish. Waiting for the gland
To dispose of the radioactive iodine,
And suchlike tediums, I visit a tea-shop
Conveniently under the crude shadow of County Hall,
Close to where Wordsworth found the earth most fair.
Coffee and bun; tea and toast; *The Times* then
The *Evening Standard,* punctuated by
The Freud Journal of Lou Andreas-Salomé.
Already one's actions smack of the legendary,
If only to oneself, since at the moment
The springs of verse are flowing after a long
Spell of being bunged up. It scarcely needed
The slimy tentacles of the cardiograph
Or the sting of the syringe's proboscis to release them.
They would have been satisfied to observe a waitress
Making sure of her lipstick before going off duty,
To mark the desolation here of the new
Concrete, and rudimentary roundabout,
Or just to read how in woman the genital zone
Is merely leased from the anal; and that (in Lou's view)
She is the antithesis of Faustian man –
For why should she pursue the unattainable
Since she herself is the goal?
                              Though immersed in the body –
Its plea to Knife and Drug, ludicrous powers,
To restore the health of youth – my Faustian aim
Is really this faeces-loving, this bourgeois

Collection and comparison of things.
Enough that the pigeon's eye blinks as slowly as
An old-fashioned camera-shutter, and that its closure
Appears to be effected by the same
Adumbrated arrangement of wrinkled stuff.
And yet uneasily I'm reminded that only
By a concession wrested from the gods
In their weak moments as swan-lovers or lyre-fans
Was art accorded the privilege of addressing
A world in which one order felt ill at ease.

Bridge and river, how did you come to be
Such strange companions? Were the grassy banks,
Separated lovers, in need of a restless creation
To mingle their gravels and really enclose the silver
Serpent forever slipping from their grasp?
Unlucky conjunction, that allowed the horsemen
To make the librarians flee, and far products
Feed local manufactories of caste.
But even when the arching stone is broken,
As it will be, and the water divides once more,
And squatting birds, making imperial helmets of boulders,
Are truly the intelligences of the ebb-tide's litter,
The arrangement of molecules will still seem
An utter irrelevance – for what has earth
To do with the purposelessness of divinities?

And yet we imagined them. Found time
From the massing of books and gold, and the mixing of phials
For the elusive elixir of immortality,
To conceive the utterly indifferent giants
In their castle of great fires and freezing corridors.
Is the universal order beneath the poet's
Contempt, then? His sorrow for humanity,
And its complex and pitiful body, too deep
To be comprised in the dust and unneighbourly constellations?

[39]

One must think so, submitting to the mercy of hospitals,
Agonized over disaster to birds, and drinking
The real but small comfort of the Indian herb.

PERVERSENESS

A broken pill keeps coming out of
The bottle, almost as though
One didn't want to be cured.
Does the instinctive order life then –
Or is it, as one's assumed,
A matter of calibre,
Chance favouring the forward?

If one meant to take an overdose,
Would you still, misshapen disc,
Keep grinning against my palm?
Rather, you'd be discovered down at
The thick amber foundation
Clutched in a white hand, skulking
Among truly innocent granules.

ORDERS

All through the summer a visiting quartet –
Father and daughter blackbird, pigeon, squirrel.
Soft cluckings in the tree announce the blackbirds:
First it was him, daring the dangerous sill;
Later brought his Cordelia of the brood –
She pouting and shivering, rather remote.
Now in her nature like all other daughters
She drives him off the grapes and bread I scatter.
Slate-flat, slate-blue taffeta tail embraced by
Matronly wings, gray marbled evenly gray,
The pigeon drops draughtmen on the terrace squares,
Patrolling ceaselessly. And in the mornings,
Anxious at the window, one hand clutched at heart,
My chinless friend, with soil-crumbed neurotic nose,
And tail a brush for cleaning babies' bottles –
Disconcertingly like Sam or Sue Squirrel.

This summer, too, I saw in J. B. Bury
'That mysterious prae-Aryan foreworld' –
Not really understanding the phrase, dimly
Conceiving a life before the oil-nurtured
Legions, before the language of short, hard words,
Before the death ships, the bronze, the chalk horses,
Which now survives only as our consciousness
Of the dotty element in our natures,
Or as a tiny, round, thinly black-haired head
Called to the colours from a cretin valley,
Or as the unmemorialed existence
To which we may be doomed.
                              The quite senseless war
Through summer days will run into winter days,
The war that during my life has scarcely stopped.
And the government that I elected, like
All governments, whether elected by me

Or not, will be powerless or uncaring.
How strange that in this sphere my desire should be
Always so different from the general will!

'There is no bridge between directional time
And timeless eternity,' wrote the gloomy
German; 'between the course of history and
The existence of a divine world order.'
Though far from belief in a divinity,
One sees indeed what he meant (and perhaps there
The translator was gravelled for the right word,
As one is oneself) – for certainly what may
Be conceived to be the principles ruling
The stuff that surrounds us, they have not to do
With bird-song, bird-love, the propulsion of metal
Into men. And what but the material
Can ever confront us, its open constants
Expressed on inevitably baffling clocks?

But I am thankful, on the whole, for this chance
To share in irrelevant events – being
In any case borne on to a species of
Significance by the drives of a motive
(No doubt falling far short of the eternal)
That will change my egotistic young blackbird
Next year to a care-worn mother. Take note, you
Gods, how my boyhood began with my father
Reading the news of the killing of young men;
How my adult body struggled with a mind
At odds with the task an unjust world imposed
And broke out in lesions that the mind despised.
Goethe said: 'The idea always appears
As a strange guest in actuality . . . The
Idea and common actuality
Must be kept strictly separate.' Very well:
Assign the business of being a poet

[43]

To an order of things entirely divine,
And the anguish to its historical material;
And accept the consolation (in Kafka's terms)
Of a wound that precisely fits the arrow.

But suppose the divinities relented,
Said: 'Your existence shall accord with our wills' –
Would our being prove even more frightening?
What would the creatures cry out at our windows,
Dark on a sky of furnace yellows: 'Join us
In the dumbness of utterly pure feeling,
To the forces that stretch you out over time
Surrender, and rejoice in the cellular
Mishaps that must bring about your extinction'?

And what if ourselves became divine, and fell
On the pitiful but attractive human,
Taking the temporary guise of a swan
Or a serpent: could we return to our more
Abstract designs untouched by the temporal;
Would we not afterwards try to get back those
Beautiful offspring, so mortal, so fated?

VARIATION ON A THEME BY SANDARS

'All our birds are capable of flight,'
Said Edmund Sandars in his *Bird Book*
For the Pocket. What a relief to
Think that nowhere on these islands are
Birds with mere elbows, or too stout birds.
It makes one, like some woman poet, want
To clap one's hands so that from grimy
Red chimney-pots, white cliffs, marshlands by
Power stations, mangy-lion moors
Rise up flung lassos, particle clouds,
Turning oscilloscope traces of
Wings; though doubtless superfluous thus
To test our author's observation.

THE VISITORS

Powers that seem to arrive from elsewhere, I
Bewilderedly open the door to you, though
I sent out the invitations and, indeed,
Recognize the visages from a lifetime's
    Dreaming of dining with gods.

No one could be more suspicious than I of
The sudden appearance of divinities
In middle-aged verse, but how else to describe
The double nature of nature in epochs
    Of creative happiness?

Besides, little use to recall, strolling at
Dusk on the suburban common with my thoughts
And walking-stick, as I stumble over the
Dung of lions, that in fact in this place a
    Circus encamped some days past.

And the tragedies of our infancy, a
Degree more real than the howl of the guilty
King, we rehearse till our death. No wonder They
Visit us sometimes to remind us of our
    Right to be blessed and consoled.

Well, enigmatic beings, though you lurk in
The gloom of book-shelves and vibrate from the grooves
Of whirling discs, I resolve to devote your
Imparting of blinding connections to those
    Who would spurn the locales.

And assert that your order, somewhat concerned
For our world, demands the expropriation
Of all whose motives are ruled by the fetish
Of things and not by the hominids who at
    Times can enchant even you.

[46]

I don't suppose you ever try to enter
The chain-hung doors of terrible rooms where the
Plotting of our downfall goes on. No, it's just
Us you can help, and our enemies frighten
 You more than they do ourselves.

And you never conceived of a species whose
Members could injure each other. In your land
The jealousies and hates cannot matter in
The end because of your immortality.
 That's what you try to confer.

UNDERGROUND GOD

When the ground was dug for the steel, glass-clad cube,
Turned up a gigantic hand. The workmen,
Mystified, brought it to the foreman; then
Students with tea-spoons unearthed a temple site.

We were amazed to find, not that the city
Had faith once, but owned a choice of deities.
Now in our office, whose casements do not open,
Whose tenants are legal fictions, we ponder such things.

Jill, Carol, Lana, succession of innocents
Straight from school, substitute Muses in
A philistine age, we search your lucid features
For signs of adhesion to one sect or the other.

Sly god of decadent empires, you were here
Already, your altars reeking of blood and semen,
During the rational century and its long
Industrious and continent aftermath –

Unknown to everyone except a few
Bedlam'd nobles, rippers in dark ginnels,
And theorists of nation-outflanking horse.
Under the drains waited your great welcoming grasp.

What forces now can your opponent put
Into the field? The gormless labourers;
Watchers of pulchritude undestined for art;
And, as in nature, autumns strangely prolonged?

DISASTERS

Can they be part of our dreams, so disastrous
They wake us, and stay in our life of waking?
Just as the assassin's shell, pitched from a world
Of black suns, and wireless voices in the head,
Comes to lodge in a situation of blood-
    Stained skirts and hopeless sorrow.

Or is it simply not true, the sense we have
Of a life ruined by us, unprompted by
Pre-existing paradigms? Didn't in fact
Primaeval fluids hold terrors for newly
Created proteins about to find out how
    To perpetuate themselves?

And galaxies move in fear of colliding?
But try to conceive the author of a whole
Hierarchy of unease; ineptness, no,
Nor malevolence could account for the lack
Of allegiance of an entire order
    To the rules that expound it.

One sees how legends came to be invented
Of gods, so to speak, picking their noses while
The dolls they'd made tore off each other's fingers,
Or of an atrocious angel whose revolt
Put the divine omnipotence for ever
    At the issue of gunfire.

But such is the rudimentary prattle
Of those whose very birth implanted a sense
Of disgust for their origin. Protest rises
From sunsets cobbled by exploded islands;
Plumage in children's water-colour oblongs;
    From fountain, doorway, rose.

Early in these November mornings, who'll dare,
Passing by portraits of worried-over love,
To open curtains on a world still dark, still
Doubtful of blackbird chinkings, moon-livid still?
The mildly-drugged with coffee and self-regard,
   Language-infatuated!

Symbolist Creator, would we have had you
Leave less to chance and speculation? How else
Except through flight along the margin of the
Permanent, heaving thing could its nature have
So imprinted itself in our sternum pulse
   And arches of our insteps?

Nymphs come from goodness knows what shrines, messages
Between their gravity-neutralising breasts:
What does it matter, even death and failure,
Utter impossibility of knowing
Their god, so long as a lifetime's aperçus
   Are unsafely recorded?

And the fires lick the violas' bellies,
Algebras lost past recall, great men dateless.
In viable atmospheres breathed on rondures
Far off, the same griefs delicately inflate,
Walking hills like mist, fogging the alleyways
   Of heroic city-states.

GODDESS

Only brown hair, he thought – as though the disguised
Goddess shouldn't have owned human attributes.
   But what other point, after
   All, had her startling entry?

It would have been an improbable, not to
Say undivine idea had she assumed
   Even a golden fleece or
   A bird's total sootiness –

Let alone masks she was capable of, as
She looked down and, at the sight of *anthropos,*
   Felt her unapproachable
   And icy nature relent.

Besides, it was part of the design that he
Should fail to identify his visitor;
   Though he drew from their fleeting
   Transactions not only luck

But also a chill sense of the purpose for
Which his lust was being employed, of her mere
   Acting of yielding's part; of
   Luck, yes, but more of mishap.

THOSE OF PURE ORIGIN

After a throbbing night, the house still dark, pull
Back the curtains, see the cherry standing there –
Grain of the paper under wash of rain-clouds.

No, our disguises are not intended to
Deceive. On the contrary. And could you name
Us we shouldn't be compelled to appear so
Confusingly – smothered in white stars, whistling
Hymn tunes, putting out scaly paws to attract
Attention. Under comic aliases –
Even the specific for insomnia:
Peppermint, lime blossom, betony, scullcap –
We entice you into our dissident realms.
The staggering plots you invent in hours
Abbreviated by anxiety are
Hatched by our logic. Just as when you try to
Talk with the girl of fifteen we tilt her shoe
Inward to imply her different order.

For it's *your* world we're expounding. Don't mistake
Our endeavours. We can't tell you where you're from.
Indeed, despite our immanence we're the last
Who could reveal more than is there already.

Let alone where you're going! Darwin's infant
Enquired about his friend's father: 'Where does
He do his barnacles?' – assumption of a
Universal preoccupation no more
Naive than yours, whether of indifference or
Concern. It's quite plausible that the concept
Of outside disappears outside – in that place
Where nebulae no longer have to awake
And pretend to be happy.

Our advice is:
Prefer the less likely explanation.
Different evenings, the evening star appearing
In different corners of the pane – conceive
No senseless revolution in the heavens
But a lucky change of erotic fortune;
A goddess steeped not in urine but in love.
And then so often you've been wrong why shouldn't
You be wrong about the extinction of man?

It's true we tend to avoid you, fatal as
You are in general to our fragility.
But sometimes one of us, whom you knew in flight
And particularly admired for his looks,
Lies down and allows the wind to blow the wrong way
His once glossy pinions. Look into his eye.
It regards you still, though fixed as well on worlds
More real than at that moment you can bear.
Of course, you'll soon take your spade and among
Pebbles, lapis worms, inter the eye from sight.

'Considering my present condition,
I can neither concentrate on poetry
Nor enjoy poetry.' That final letter
May seem a defeat after a lifetime of
Assuming the reality of the art.
Not to us, though it's we are the defeated.
For we boast of our patience – coral *croissants*
Anchored at last to just too-heavy hill-tops;
Laboratories of finches; Galapagos
Of revelation awaiting an observer.
And you, even in the children's puzzle, are
You certain you've seen all the hidden objects?

Yes, there's the extrusion of the wall in
A clawed hump, and a grey frayed rope-end blown round
And round a bough. But what are the abstract shapes
As enigmatic in significance as
Those painters find incised from oceans by arcs
Of a parasol or enclosed from a beach
By the severe bay of a young throat and jaw?

That countenance whose eyes are as pale as if
The flesh had been clipped out to show the ash sky
Behind it . . . The voice that unavailingly
Says: 'Do you remember taking your laundry
To the woman with elephant legs?' . . . The past
As ambiguous as hailstones in the gales
Of Spring: the future certain – the instant when
You stop being convinced of our existence,
And meaningless that blackbirds masquerade as owls,
That also in the dusk, making free of it
For assignations, jealousies (those affairs
Of energy and waiting unwearying,
Of obsession with menstrual blood), occur
The strange pre-marital flights of humans.

What does it matter that the baptistery proves
As dusty and void as bad nuts when its doors
Provide a progression of style, the basher
Of bronze breaking out from pious platitudes
Into arcades of applied geometry,
Thronged with our perfect but realistic forms?

The mad poet called us, untranslatably:
'Those of pure origin' – left you to divine
Whether we rise from phenomena or,
Perhaps more likely, also require your presence,
As the cathedral the plague, pity the war.

[54]

But how can we pretend our hemisphere-wide
Lament, the random trickling and joining of tears
On acres of glass, is entirely for your
Predicament – as your lives, borne upon the
More and more dubiously physical, move
To regions of abnegation and concern
Whose angels we are; though, under cruel casques,
Our curls, our thick, parted lips ever youthful,
Complexions marked with still unmalignant moles
Of the actual, scabs on unfolding leaves?

AFTERNOONS

Mothers with taller daughters, shopping
In afternoons, what sustains your lives?
Here's a pair of crimson plastic lips
Left over from a Christmas cracker:
To which generation shall I offer it?

Conceived after the last of wars that surely
Could possibly lead to works of art,
Shall these saplings be hacked down?

Like bluebells in a wood the uniforms
Through the palace railings. Some insane inscription
Cut from a poet's elegy
Identifies the ill-horsed author of carnage.

De-birding jelly, black with grime, on the shaven
Polls of the persians – a savage concept of coiffure –
Has failed to shift the sense of a plaza
Snowing with fragments of brain, the pavement stained;
Debris of an exploded urban dream.

Towers strike out the time for tea,
The time of rehearsals, the time before
The hard liquor of old age. Come in
From your gazing at stockings long as prunus boughs
For almost calfless legs,
And open patterns for knitted bed-jackets
To the jangling of guitars. Poor Gorgons –
Doomed to decapitation in the very
Instant of parturition; the question is
How to prolong your breeding
Of the Muses' continually defeated favourites.

WINDOWS

Easy to tell how habitually I
Look through these great spectacles that enlarge the
Soul's eye – so that sunsets, for instance, of quite
Undifferentiated madder seem to
Possess the glamour of unapproachable
Geniuses, in an existence apart.

Sometimes the sky has a ghostly lampshade or
Countenance watermarked in it, as if it
Were making abundantly plain its divorce
From phenomena; for although the lenses
Intensify perception, to the object
Their attitude is deeply ambiguous.

Should a bird come out of the darkly-banked trees and
Alight on a seat's conveniently bent
Arm, one sees that its pupil (if a pigeon)
Is not, as one thought, the core of a target
But oblate, as though to keep tripping, while it
Revolves, some shaft from a dangerous image.

And one's fingers against the pane are stopped, by
A force that whitens the nails, from seizing the
Dove in their grasp. How tender the world outside
Seems to be, how full of things one could adore –
Were it removed, then, this manner of vision,
Should I fall in the wings of a vast embrace?

Or rather a climate of lunar harshness
Wither my hopes? These tears on the glass are shed
From beings outside with sorrows so huge as
To overwhelm our pity; and not even
Our miniature fires are really printed
On the darkness that incessantly comes down.

DEPARTURES

No, I'll not let you go yet, sweetest
Girl, though you ache to depart from my
Boring house, where you're fed with the crumbs
Of experience, loved with the most
    Perfunctory of kisses.

I've something still to tell, if only,
As to a comfortable old wife,
The trivial news of the day, how
I avoided drowning an insect
    In the lavatory at dawn –

Where cyclamen leaves on the lighter
Tone of the window brought to mind the
Lotus in those banal surroundings
That the hour made mysterious;
    Prince Buddha in the passage.

Or perhaps you'll reveal to me why,
Say, the well-concealed Schoenbergian
Mathematics of art have meaning
In the actual intervals, and
    Tremblings of the finger-pads.

As you make a tough, Guinness-drinking
Quintet aware of an odd man out:
That flautist, is he the emperor
Or even perhaps the composer,
    Playing too many wrong notes?

Unworthy to receive your embrace,
I'm always resolving to do much
Better in future, an eternal
Unsatisfactory boy; somehow
    Believing that I will, too.

[58]

Possibly I'll dare to write my last
Songs for soprano. Certainly, you –
Exciting and wholly unexplored
Landscape of secret features – sometimes
    Hold out encouragement.

And even when all else fails, the child
That emerged from my truest because
Uncritically accepting life
Will blessedly know of your demands
    And help warrant the future.

For you can't pass in the street, as though
You didn't know them, quite all my race.
Dear Muse, as I grow older you get
More desirable, and in your youth
    (Theoretically free)

You tantalise with the innocence
Of the unpossessed; even the cross
Between your slight breasts seems to render
The transcendental a prey of the
    Conceivably possible.

Besides, since you represent the whole
Human world, your being continues
Apart from the favours you fail to
Bestow, and it matters not at all
    That your slave weeps in his room.

Yes, it's only the deprived who can
Appreciate the beautiful life
Of the entirely committed to
Providing an area in which
    Wrong proteins can make marvels.

[59]

Future readers, whose predecessors
Expectedly neglect me, may find
I spoke truly of our posthumous
Life they are enjoying, because of
    My dull faithfulness to you.

What cosy times we've had together,
Playing the gramophone, sipping scotch
And soda; and I very often
Not even getting as far as the
    Nylon cords behind your knee.

Apples are clinging to yellow boughs,
Fruit that the birds have made
Decayed moons; in the false cover of
Fallen leaves, pink worms: drapes just meeting
    Across the stage of corpses.

We look to you to bring to cities'
Repetitive machinery skies
Of marine splendour behind marble
Porticos where Baudelairean
    Hand-maids are already nude.

But should it be thus that the body,
Otiosely ill and naturally
Deficient, appeals to a goddess
It knows to be a figment of its
    Death or of its thoughts of death?

No, the best should await with humble
And excited awe your routine calls,
And dogged life itself must tempt you
To descend, or whirl to remotest
    Quasars in flurries of apes.

LAST SHEET

. . . Suddenly it's autumn, I think, as I look in the garden –
A gloomy dripping world, tree-tops lost in cloud.
Is it possible that anyone so silly can
Write anything good? I don't hear, like poor Virginia,
The birds outside the window talking Greek. I see
My blackbird visitor and wonder where he sleeps,
As sleep he must. And catch my face in the pane,
Becoming ancestral, a cartoon of the mask
To which I've always been indulgent. And turn
To put a disc of Debussy on the machine:
This is what I'd have written had I had genius.
A pity to have got so far along the road
And then never arrived. Give my regards to the Minister
And tell him I've drafted a comprehensive instrument
For the administration of suburbia.

This is the time the robin starts to sing at dusk,
Like a cog catching on cardboard, but the human throat
Is not subject to seasons except those of the withering heart.
They're trying to cure me of my maladjusted glands –
Amusing; rather like trying to change the art of Sickert:
'I've always been a literary painter,
Thank goodness, like all decent painters,' he said.
One can joke, but nevertheless the situation is tragic –
A human lifetime's limited store of eggs, and then
Their very last descent into the longing womb.
It's certainly on the cards that I shall never write
Another letter. This will have to stand, as usual,
For the prodigies I was about to tell you of,
For the connections I never quite saw, the melodies
Played gently while the beauteous statue reconciled
The jarred generations, and Sicily and Bohemia.

[61]